Lessons Learned from Jonah

Lessons Learned from Jonah

Meditations on God's Restoring Grace

ROBERT SNITKO

Foreword by Dan Jacobsen

RESOURCE *Publications* · Eugene, Oregon

LESSONS LEARNED FROM JONAH
Meditations on God's Restoring Grace

Resource Publications
An Imprint of Wipf and Stock Publishers
199 W. 8th Ave., Suite 3
Eugene, OR 97401

www.wipfandstock.com

PAPERBACK ISBN: 978-1-5326-3347-8
HARDCOVER ISBN: 978-1-5326-3349-2
EBOOK ISBN: 978-1-5326-3348-5

Manufactured in the U.S.A.   AUGUST 23, 2017

For Mags.
Thank you for your persistent,
Christ-like love towards me.

Contents

Foreword

The devotional you hold in your hands is rather unique. For starters, it has a unique author. The first time I met Rob was when he walked into my office as a summer intern after his first year in college. It didn't take long for me to be impressed by two things—his love of Jesus and his impressive work ethic. Rob's story and life have been marked by a radical love for Jesus in ways that can only be attributed to the work of the Holy Spirit in him. All the more, in an age where acceptable study methods consist of typing questions into Google, Rob has committed himself to hard work of deep, thoughtful, and labor intensive study of Scripture without shortcuts. That you will find yourself in these lessons is proof of Rob's ability to understand and communicate well.

I also appreciate this devotional for its unique perspective. Studies in the Minor Prophets have a tendency toward moralism and allegorization. You won't find that here. With a Spurgeon-esque approach of taking the text straight to the cross, the points of the text are allowed to become pointers to Christ. Why more devotions don't take this approach is a mystery. After all, this is the approach Jesus himself takes in Matthew's gospel, as he reinterprets the Jonah prophecy to be ultimately understood through the lens of his own life, death, and resurrection (Matthew 12:38–42).

This approach makes these lessons invaluable to the new Christian as well as the seasoned saint.

The combination of a unique author with a unique perspective ultimately yields a work with a unique goal: transformation. These lessons are not designed to leave us where we started. In wrestling with the immediate story of Jonah and the wider story of Redemption, we are forced to consider those areas of our lives that need refinement and progress.

As you read these lessons, I'm sure you will, like me, admire Rob's pastoral heart, helpful guidance, and ability to demystify the story in a way that speaks to our real lives today.

Dan Jacobsen
Campus Pastor
Bethel Church

Acknowledgments

I would like to thank my incredible wife, Mags, for constantly encouraging me to write, while challenging me in my thinking as I write. Thank you for noticing the irresistible grace of God that is found in the Jonah narrative. This work would not have transpired without your insight and diligence for God and His love towards people. I would also like to thank my brother-in-law, Ben, for being a second pair of eyes during this writing process. Your push for excellence in writing is very admirable. Finally, thank you to all who continue to support me in this journey called life. You know who you are. May the Lord bless you as the gospel of Christ dwells within you.

Introduction

The narrative of Jonah is most commonly known as the book about the man inside of a whale. But it is much more than that. In fact, Jonah is one of the most profound stories that we find throughout the entire Bible. It illustrates who we are as fallen human beings, along with our sinful tendencies to run away from God in the moments that He calls us to obedience. The book of Jonah is loaded with God's grace which continues to pursue us, even in the midst of our rebellion and selfishness. Despite Jonah's self-seeking and self-serving heart, God, faithfully sought him out. This is because our God is one of grace, love, and forgiveness. In Him, we find comfort, peace, and encouragement, as He never gives up on us, even when we are focused on ourselves.

The reality is that we all chase self-preservation. However, through Jonah's story, God shows that He is merciful to us in the midst of our selfish pursuits, providing grace upon grace so that we may experience His love towards us. Even though we constantly fall short of the *glory* of God (Romans 3:23), there is hope for us in fulfilling the *will* of God. That hope is found in the faithfulness of God who offers to us His Son, Jesus Christ, so that we may experience the riches of His love.

I was inspired to write this devotional because of my passion for the book of Jonah, and because there is much to be learned from studying the ways that we are similar—and dissimilar—to Jonah. Each devotion will conclude with Christological implications for us today. In other words, each one will wrap up with thoughts on how the gospel meets us in the midst of our situations. The gospel is the good news that nourishes us and sustains us. These Christological implications will allow us to see how God covers us in His grace through and through, even when we fall short time and time again.

The grace of God brings restoration and healing for all who are suffering and broken. The grace of God is never-ending as it displays in the Jonah narrative. God pursues Jonah, the sailors, and the Ninevites regardless of their sinful acts of rebellion towards Him. The narrative displays how the grace of God brings restoration to those who rebel against God. So, let's dive into the story and experience the wondrous love that offered from our gracious God.

PART 1

Jonah Chapter One

Stop Running, Listen

The word of the Lord came to Jonah son of Amittai: "Go to the great city of Nineveh and preach against it, because its wickedness has come up before me." But Jonah ran away from the Lord and headed for Tarshish. He went down to Joppa, where he found a ship bound for that port. After paying the fare, he went aboard and sailed for Tarshish to flee from the Lord.

JONAH 1:1–3

We live in a world that is constantly on the go. We run from one place to the next and are so used to doing so that life often becomes a blur. When we finally have a moment to catch our breath, we tend to look for another way to keep running. This is a normative Western posture in the twenty-first century, and we all participate in this lifestyle because we think it is gratifying.

So as we run from God, are we really just trying to cover up the true state of our hearts? The reality is that if we slow down, we are going to hear from God. And in hearing from God, we fear that God is going to ask us to do something that may require our utmost obedience. Are we afraid that if we slow down, God is finally going to be able to speak to us? Is this mask of busyness something that we cling to so that we don't have to deal with our hearts before God? Because if we stopped running all over the place and slowed down, God would get our attention, convict us of our sin, and perhaps even call us to something too difficult for our handling. Brothers and sisters, the joy is that no matter what God is trying to tell us, He will get us through with His grace, love, and mercy. We are not alone in this. God is completely in control and in His grace, He is calling us to stop running and start listening.

This reality hit home for Jonah. A messenger of God in the Old Testament, Jonah, was given a direct order from God so that His truth could be proclaimed boldly (Jonah 1:1–2). But Jonah decided that he knew better. Jonah paid a fare, and sailed in the complete opposite direction of where God was asking Him to go. Jonah fled from the Lord because he feared what God was asking him to do (Jonah 1:3). God wanted to use Jonah in Nineveh—a broken and desperate place—so that he could preach against the city. But Jonah, in his selfishness and fear, ran away from God.

In the midst of our running from God, Jesus Christ remains on the throne. His bloodshed has already occurred on our behalf. In our failure to stop running, God, in His grace and mercy, bestows His forgiveness to us in His Son, Jesus Christ. Jesus Christ covers our disobedient pursuit of God and His will for our lives.

CALL TO ACTION

Are you running from God? Are you afraid that God is going to ask you to do something that you may not be comfortable with? Are you living in fear? Do you know what God is asking of you, therefore you have decided to flee from Him? Often times, we run from God because we're afraid of what He may ask us to do. If that's you, I want to encourage you to pause. Take a moment to ask God for forgiveness for the fact that you continue to run from Him when He is asking you to slow down and incline your ear to Him. Ask God to speak to you so that you may understand what it is that He desires from you.

REFLECTIONS ON JONAH 1:1–3

"In the midst of our running from God,
Jesus Christ remains on the throne."

In the Midst of Storms

Then the Lord sent a great wind on the sea, and such a violent storm arose that the ship threatened to break up. All the sailors were afraid and each cried out to his own god. And they threw the cargo into the sea to lighten the ship. But Jonah had gone below deck, where he lay down and fell into a deep sleep. The captain went to him and said, "How can you sleep? Get up and call on your god! Maybe he will take notice of us so that we will not perish."

JONAH 1:4–6

When a storm comes your way, how do you respond? Do you turn to God, or do you turn to your own form of a god? When Jonah boarded the ship for Tarshish, he blatantly disobeyed the commands that God had given him. Because of Jonah's disobedience, God sent a violent storm that threatened to thrash the ship. The sailors were terrified. In their fear they each cried out to their own god, but the storm did not abate. It simply grew worse.

In the midst of the storms in our lives, do we cry out to the One True God who can heal and meet us right where we are at? Or do we cling to the idols of this world, trying to seek fulfillment in the things that replace God in our lives? What do you cling to in the midst of storms? Is it a material possession? Is it an ongoing addiction that you continue to participate in because it brings you temporary relief? To what god do you cling when you are being ravaged by the storms of this life?

God sends storms our way so that our faith in Him may be strengthened. Often, when things are going well, we don't want anything to do with God because we don't believe that we need Him. We only come to Him when we are in a difficult place. God is a jealous God (Exodus 20:4–5) and He wants our affection. The New Testament tells us that we ought to consider it pure joy when we encounter various storms in our lives, as these storms produce steadfastness and endurance in our faith (James 1:2–3). So what is God trying to do in the midst of Jonah's disobedience? God is trying to get Jonah's attention by sending a storm. Yet, Jonah refused to deal with the storm in his life, choosing instead to lie down below the deck, hoping that God forgets his disobedience.

We, too, fall short of being wholly obedient to God. We run just as Jonah ran. We hide just as Jonah hid. And God tries to get our attention by sending storms our way. Are we going to trust that He has a far greater purpose for us than we could ever imagine? What if we continue to fall short in the midst of storms? When we fail to live up to God's standards, God repeatedly displays His grace in the gospel. God accomplishes His purpose in our lives through His Son, Jesus Christ. And when we fall short, Christ will cover us. When storms come our way, God will cover us with His grace. When we lack trust and choose to go our separate way, God seeks us out and captures our attention. God is a God who constantly draws near to His people. He has united Himself to His people in Jesus Christ. And when storms come our way, the incarnation of the Son of God is our hope. Even Jesus encountered many storms in His life, and He was able to overcome them because of God's faithful grace alone.

CALL TO ACTION

What do you do in the midst of a storm? Do you cling to worthless idols, or do you hold fast to the One True God, who is eager to meet you where you are? Ask God to meet you in the storms that come your way. Know that He is patient with you and wants to give you His peace and His strength in the midst of your storm. Trust in Him.

REFLECTIONS ON JONAH 1:4-6

*"When we fail to live up to God's standards,
God repeatedly displays His grace in the gospel."*

Identity

Then the sailors said to each other, "Come, let us cast lots to find out who is responsible for this calamity." They cast lots and the lot fell on Jonah. So they asked him, "Tell us, who is responsible for making all this trouble for us? What kind of work do you do? Where do you come from? What is your country? From what people are you?" He answered, "I am a Hebrew and I worship the Lord, the God of heaven, who made the sea and the dry land."

Jonah 1:7–9

Identity is a loaded word. It is, quite literally, the definition of one's personhood. Some understand their identity within the context of their work environment. Some associate their identity with their country of origin, or where they have grown up for most of their lives. Others define their identity according to the type of people with which they associate themselves. And for the Christian, identity is found in one's faith.

As the storm continues in the Jonah narrative, the sailors begin to panic. The cries to their own gods did not calm the storm. So in order to figure out the cause of the storm, they cast lots. The lots fell on Jonah, which urged their need of an explanation. They begin to interrogate him: "Who is responsible for making all this trouble for us? What kind of work do you do? Where do you come from? What is your country? From what people are you? (Jonah 1:8)." The sailors are interested in Jonah's identity; they want to know who he really is and so they can determine the cause of the storm. Jonah replied to them, "I am a Hebrew and I worship the Lord, the God of heaven, who made the sea and dry land" (Jonah 1:9). Regardless of Jonah's disobedience, he knows to whom he belongs.

How do we determine our identity? Is it in our jobs? Our statuses? Our ethnicities? Our possessions? God created us in His image (Genesis 1:27), but we chose to rebel against God in our sinfulness, separating us from our creator. But God, in His love, sent His Son into the world that we might live through Him (1 John 4:9). In Christ, we have been crucified, thus it is no longer we who live, but Christ who lives in us (Galatians 2:20). Christian, your identity is found in Jesus Christ alone. Look no further. Grace is right before you. God has given you Salvation and a new identity—His name is Jesus.

CALL TO ACTION

When it comes to your identity, where do you look? Do you look to the unfulfilling things that this world has to offer, or do you look for your fulfillment in the Son of God, Jesus Christ, our Lord? Spend some time reflecting on the cross of Jesus Christ. In this time, reflect upon the identity that you have been given in Christ Jesus. You no longer have to seek to find your identity in any thing, in any substance, in any title. Instead, your identity has been given to you as you bear the image of God in Christ Jesus.

REFLECTIONS ON JONAH 1:7-9

"Your identity is found in Jesus Christ alone."

Our Need for God

This terrified them and they asked, "What have you done?"
(They knew he was running away from the Lord, because
he had already told them so.) The sea was getting rougher
and rougher. So they asked him, "What should we do to you
to make the sea calm down for us?" "Pick me up and throw
me into the sea," he replied, "and it will become calm. I know
that it is my fault that this great storm has come upon you."

JONAH 1:10–12

In a consumer driven culture, we always seek the next best thing.
We need the newest cell phone, the newest computer, the newest and best car that we could possibly have. This is what culture
has taught us when it comes to our needs. Contrary to the world's
standards, the Bible encourages us to recognize our utter depen-
dence on God. Not the "next best thing," but our complete depen-
dence on our Creator.

The storm persist and the sailors' terror grows. God reveals
to them that Jonah was running away from Him. What if Jonah
decided to obey God instead of running from Him? Perhaps this
storm would've never taken place. But as the sailors are barraged

by the storm, Jonah begins to understand the implications of his shortcomings. Jonah realizes that his disobedience didn't only sever his relationship with God, but his selfishness also caused the sailors to suffer (Jonah 1:12). He was not depending on God. Instead, he sought after his own desires, not realizing his need for God.

Do you have a complete need for God? Do you recognize your desperate need for God's presence? Jonah rebelled and felt the consequences of his rebellion. Jonah began to realize that he actually needed God. God desires that we seek to have a relationship with with Him. We know that when we live in a community of family and friends, we must pursue those relationships in order for them to have preservation. The same is the case when it comes to God. We need to do our part in recognizing our need for Him, so that our relationship with Him is preserved. Even though we often fail in this area, God in His goodness, forgives us in His Son. He restores us to Himself. This is why God gives us His very words, which are written in the Scriptures. These words are meant for our nourishment, edification, preservation, and sanctification. God speaks to us through the Scriptures, which causes us to yearn for Him. Be encouraged that when we fail, God will engulf us in His never-ending grace, so that we may experience a life filled with the gospel.

CALL TO ACTION

Come and freely receive the free gift of Salvation that is offered in the Lord Jesus Christ. In this gift, you will experience the depths of the love of God. The gospel will reveal your need for God. Spend some time reflecting on where you are at with God. Ask Him to enter into your space and reveal more of who He is for you.

REFLECTIONS ON JONAH 1:10–12

"Even though we often fail,
God in His goodness, forgives us in His Son."

A Life without Godliness
Is a Life of Tragedy

Instead, the men did their best to row back to land. But they could not, for the sea grew even wilder than before. Then they cried out to the Lord, "Please, Lord, do not let us die for taking this man's life. Do not hold us accountable for killing an innocent man, for you, Lord, have done as you pleased." Then they took Jonah and threw him overboard, and the raging sea grew calm. At this the men greatly feared the Lord, and they offered a sacrifice to the Lord and made vows to him.

Jonah 1:13–16

How tragic would it be if this world was without God? What if there was never healing for our pain? Or restoration for our brokenness? What if God decided to let us be eternally separated from Him, not being able to know Him? But that is not God because God is love. God revealed Himself to us and has made Himself known. Because of this, we can experience His fullness through the gospel of Christ.

Let's shift gears here for a moment. Instead of focusing on Jonah, let's focus on the sailors in this section. The sailors did everything that they could to avoid the storm. They cried out to their gods. They threw cargo off of their ship. They even tried their hardest to row back to the land, but they couldn't because the sea raged even more than before (Jonah 1:13). They were living a life that did not involve God. Instead, they tried to save themselves of their own accord. No matter what they did, things only got worse. This provoked the sailors to do the only thing that was left for them to do: they cried out the Lord, the Creator of all things, the Creator of the land and of the sea upon which they sailed. Their fear led them to a realization that in the midst of their fear and failure, the One True God is the only One who would hear their cries.

What would life be like if we were completely separated from God? How tragic it would be if God turned His back on us! The good news is that this will never be the case for those who love the Lord. God never intended for us to be separated from Him. Despite our tendency to flee from the Lord and seek for other things to fulfill us, He constantly pursues our very hearts. The sailors were neck deep in their sin, yet God, in His sovereign grace, still chose to reveal Himself to them. They realized that the storm that they were in was far too great for them to conquer on their own. And God knows that your life is far too difficult to conquer on your own. This is why God has given us His Son, Jesus Christ. God has gifted us with His Son so that we don't have to do this life on our own. When we fail to chase after God, He will chase after us. God is constantly pursuing us because He is longing to be in communion with us. So will you partake of this gospel? Will you allow the gospel of grace and love to transform the way you live as it transformed the lives of the sailors. Repent and believe in Christ, and the Lord God will give you rest. He calmed the storm for the sailors and He will calm the storms you are facing.

CALL TO ACTION

Where are you at in your relationship with God? Wherever you are, know that God is looking to restore your relationship with Him. Even if you are wayward, God is faithful to pursue you. Ask God for forgiveness for your tendency to neglect Him. Repent of your sin and seek healing in the cross of Jesus Christ. Seek God and ask Him to equip you with everything that you need to participate in godly living. Seek God to make the gospel known in your life, each and every day.

"When we fail to chase after God, He will chase after us."

God's Sovereign Provision

Now the Lord provided a huge fish to swallow Jonah, and
Jonah was in the belly of the fish three days and three nights.

JONAH 1:17

It is unquestionable that every human being desires some form
of comfort. But the question is, where will we go for comfort
when we are faced with adversity? We can either trust that God has
a plan for us, or we can look elsewhere for answers. The question
remains, how can we find comfort in God's sovereign provision?

After experiencing God, the sailors put their confidence in
Him, knowing that He would protect Jonah, as they threw him
overboard. They did this because they trusted that God would
provide a way for Jonah to survive. Jonah himself, knew that this
was going to be the only way that the storm would calm. So the
sailors took Jonah and tossed him into the sea and immediately, a
large fish swallowed Jonah, and Jonah resided in the fish for three
days and three nights (Jonah 1:17). It seemed as if this was the end
for Jonah. How could one be hurled into a raging sea and survive
the massive storm? God showed up in the midst of Jonah's disobedience and provided a large fish to swallow Jonah up. God's

sovereign provision was over Jonah as God sought to protect Jonah from harm. God provided a way out for Jonah.

Are you in a place where everything seems hopeless? Are you lost and feel like you can't be found? Or are you in a place where you feel like giving up? Rest assured that God is bigger than any situation. God is willing to meet you where you are at so that you may encounter His grace towards you. Did you know that God is constantly offering up His grace in every circumstance? Just as Jonah's situation seemed hopeless and discouraging, that his life was coming to an end, he was entering into the depths of God's grace. God displayed His grace by providing a large fish to swallow Jonah and protect him from the sea.

As soon as Jonah was thrown overboard, the storm calmed. This was the result of God's care for the sailors and His care for Jonah's situation. Can you relate to Jonah's situation? Do you feel like you're in the depths of raging waters? Whether or not that's you, know that God is providing comfort to you in the gospel of Christ. Christ is ever satisfying as He nourishes us with His broken body and shed blood. When you worry, Christ is enough. When you fear, Christ is enough. When you hunger, Christ is enough. When you thirst, Christ is enough. When you're drowning, Christ is enough. He will provide a way for you to encounter God's sovereign provision for you.

CALL TO ACTION

Christian, are you weary? Are you doubting? Are you exhausted? Allow the gospel of Jesus Christ to penetrate your spirit. Find your forgiveness in Christ Jesus, who will heal you in your circumstance. He is all you need. Acknowledge that Christ is all you need and allow God to reshape your thinking, so that you may be forever changed. The gospel is God's sovereign provision for your life. Will you partake?

REFLECTIONS ON JONAH 1:17

*"Christ is ever satisfying as He nourishes us
with His broken body and shed blood."*

PART 2

Jonah Chapter Two

In My Distress

From inside the fish Jonah prayed to the Lord his God. He said: "In my distress I called to the Lord, and he answered me. From deep in the realm of the dead I called for help, and you listened to my cry.

JONAH 2:1–2

L ife can often be distressing. We feel the anxieties that come with day-to-day life. We feel the weight of sorrow throughout its various seasons. Our flesh is weak and, more often than not, we need supernatural strength in order to get through another day. What is the cause of all of this? Our suffering is a result of our fallen human nature. We experience these distresses as a direct result of the sin that has entered into this world.

After the sailors throw Jonah into the sea, God provides a safe place for him in the belly of a large fish. Clearly, Jonah is distressed because of the weight of his disobedience. Stuck in the belly of the fish, he calls out to the Lord in prayer. Perhaps Jonah was afraid and anxious because of his current situation of being in the belly of the fish, not knowing what was ahead of him. Maybe he was ashamed and sorrowful because of the situation that he put the sailors in: knowing that it was because of his disobedience others suffered. But Jonah knew that God listened to his plea.

Like Jonah, we ought to cry out to our heavenly Father in the midst of our distress. God is faithful to listen and—in His timing— answer. Christian, know that you're not alone in your distress. For God has incarnated Himself into the very humanity that you and I partake in. He became flesh and dwelt among us (John 1:14). He experienced the distresses that this world brought with it. The Son of God experienced the temptations (Matthew 4:1–11). Jesus Christ experienced sorrow, to the point of death (Matthew 26:38). He experienced fear and anxiety at the Garden of Gethsemane, as He was pleading with our heavenly Father to take this burden away from Him (Matthew 26:39). The burden of dying on a cross for you and for me. Brothers and sisters, Jesus Christ has experienced the distresses of humanity in His very own humanity. And not only did He experience these distresses, He conquered them. Jesus Christ conquered distress on the cross at Calvary. Because not only did He conquer them on the cross by taking our distresses to the cross with Him, but Jesus Christ conquered the grave and gave us hope for life everlasting. In the midst of your distress, look to the cross. See that it is empty. And rejoice in Christ. Because Christ has come to conquer your distress. Believe in Him and allow Him to meet you in your distress.

CALL TO ACTION

Spend some time writing down the distresses that are in your midst. Is it anxiety? Is it pain? Is it sorrow? What is weighing you down right now? Offer these things up to the Lord and allow His gospel to purify your distresses. Trust in His grace and His mercy. For His grace and mercy is given to you this day.

REFLECTIONS ON JONAH 2:1-2

*"Jesus Christ conquered the grave and
gave us hope for life everlasting."*

The Power of Lament

You hurled me into the depths, into the very heart of the seas, and the currents swirled about me; all your waves and breakers swept over me. I said, 'I have been banished from your sight; yet I will look again toward your holy temple.' The engulfing waters threatened me, the deep surrounded me; seaweed was wrapped around my head.

JONAH 2:3–5

Christians are often discouraged to lament because we view lament as a weakness or a "lack of faith." How could a Christian lament if God is on their side? Aren't Christians always supposed to be happy and content? This couldn't be further from the truth. Christians are human beings. We all experience emotions. And God has given us emotions so that we could express them. Especially, so that we could express our emotions towards Him.

In the depths of Jonah's distress he lamented. Jonah understood the weight of his wrongdoing. He knew that God had hurled him into the depths of the seas, and he feared for his life as he was out in the middle of nowhere. But as Jonah was being tossed and turned by the waves, God saved him. This caused Jonah to cry out to God in lament, knowing that he wronged God. Knowing that lamenting would allow God to know exactly how he felt. Jonah, in the belly of the large fish, lamented to God.

The only thing that is different between a non-Christian and a Christian is that Christians, by God's grace, are able to recognize that they are sinners in need of a Savior. Lament is a spiritual discipline that all ought to partake in. What are the things that bring us sorrow? What are the things that bring us pain? Whatever these things may be, we are encouraged to lament. Lamenting is a way to passionately express ourselves before God. Our prayers do not have to be dry or bland. Instead, when we come before a holy God, we ought to express ourselves to Him in the most authentic way we can. Jonah wholeheartedly shared his concerns with God to the point of lament. Not wanting to be killed for the sins of the world, but knowing that God's will takes precedence over His desires, even Jesus lamented at the garden of Gethsemane. At the cross, He cried out, "My God, My God, why have you forsaken me?" (Matthew 27:46). Jesus was always genuine and honest before His Father in heaven. There was power in the lament of Christ. Likewise, we have been given the freedom to lament. In our lament, God is glorified.

CALL TO ACTION

Where are you at today? Are you being led to lament before God? Are you afraid to be transparent before God and before others? Brothers and sisters, call out to God. Call out to God with your emotions. Do not be afraid. Go in a space where you can be alone with God. Tell Him where your heart truly is. And ask Him to meet you in your lament towards Him. Once you have done so, reflect on your experience of time spent in lament.

REFLECTIONS ON JONAH 2:3–5

"We have been given the freedom to lament."

Worship

To the roots of the mountains I sank down; the earth beneath barred me in forever. But you, Lord my God, brought my life up from the pit. "When my life was ebbing away, I remembered you, Lord, and my prayer rose to you, to your holy temple. "Those who cling to worthless idols turn away from God's love for them. But I, with shouts of grateful praise, will sacrifice to you. What I have vowed I will make good. I will say, 'Salvation comes from the Lord.'"

JONAH 2:6–9

This world has a lot to offer when it comes to whom or what we worship. We can choose to worship many gods: technology, our careers, our family and friends (just to name a few). But none of these things are ever going to fully satisfy. In fact, they will disappoint, time and time again. So how do we worship? Better yet, whom do we worship?

Jonah is still residing in the belly of the fish and having an ongoing conversation with God. Repenting of his sin and lamenting to God, he expresses his gratefulness to God for sparing his life. Jonah was sinking into the deep and God brought his life up from the pit. He called out to God from the ocean's depths and God saved him. In response, Jonah praises God in his prayer, telling God that he (Jonah) remembered Him, as he was ebbing away. Jonah also contrasts his situation by expressing to God that he shouted grateful praise, while those who cling to worthless idols will not experience God's love for them (Jonah 2:8). Salvation comes from the Lord and Jonah began to realize the importance of this reality. In doing so, Jonah mustered up courage and was ready to fulfill God's call. Jonah's experience in the large fish was transformative; he affirmed his love for God as he began to shout great praise to the Lord.

Do we find ourselves worshipping false and worthless idols? Or do we long to lift praises to the One True God? It is easy to fall short and fall into the temptation of worshipping false gods. We must seek to forsake these gods. When it comes to our worship, we ought to examine ourselves before the Lord and let the Holy Spirit discern our motives. The gods in our lives can easily take control, but we must forsake the worthless idols that exist in our lives and shift our focus to worshipping the name of Jesus Christ. Fixing our eyes on Christ will help us flee from fixing our eyes on anything else. This is who Jesus is. He is here for our nourishment by offering Himself as ultimate nourishment. Jesus is here to fully satisfy us in Himself by offering us His flesh and blood (John 6:53). If we partake in His flesh and blood, we will have life. When we worship other gods, Jesus enters into our presence to redirect our hearts and thoughts towards Him. Will you worship Jesus Christ alone?

CALL TO WORSHIP

Who or what are you worshipping? Does your worship need to be redefined? Christian, allow the gospel of Christ Jesus to bring you rest and peace in Himself. Find your worth and value in Christ and Christ alone. Worship His holy and matchless name forevermore. Spend some time reflecting on how Jesus is all fulfilling and all satisfying.

*"Fixing our eyes on Christ will help us flee
from fixing our eyes on anything else."*

PART 3

Jonah Chapter Three

Second Chances

And the Lord commanded the fish, and it vomited Jonah onto dry land. Then the word of the Lord came to Jonah a second time: "Go to the great city of Nineveh and proclaim to it the message I give you."

JONAH 2:10 — 3:2

We fail time and time again in the many tasks and responsibilities that life brings our way. We fall short of the goals that we set. We fall short in how we spend time with friends and family. We even fall short in our walk with God. So often we are discouraged in our time spent with God. Whether it's a lack of time in the scriptures, or a lacking prayer life, we experience the reality of "falling short."

After facing many trials, Jonah realized the implications of his disobedience to God. Jonah spent three days and three nights inside of the fish. But God, in His grace, provided Jonah with a second chance. God was working on Jonah's restoration within the belly of the fish. This was a space that Jonah was able to reflect on his life and on why he landed in such a situation. God used Jonah's failures to bring Jonah to Himself. And during this time in the whale, Jonah understood that God is faithful to grant second chances.

The same is true for us. God is a God of second chances. This is the reason that He sent His Son, Jesus Christ, into the world. Jesus came to give us a second chance in life because if it were up to us, we would fail over and over again. The truth of the matter is that we do—even as Christians—fail, time and time again. We fail in our pursuit of God. We fail in our desire to know God more. We fail at trying to read our Bibles on a daily basis. We fail to pray as often as we wish we could. But our hope is not in our success. Our hope is in Christ, who takes away our failures in Himself. He takes our fallen nature and redeems it through His resurrection. Christ proved to us that He defeated the grave (1 Corinthians 15:55–57) and has overcome death. Therefore Christ is faithful to overcome our failures and our shortcomings. God, in His love, sent Jesus to overcome our failures. This is our hope in second chances. But what happens if we fail in our second chances? Christ gives us a third chance, and a fourth chance, and a fifth chance, and so on. Why? Because Jesus forgives sinners. And we are sinners. Let us rest in His saving grace in the midst of the failures that come our way, for He is faithful to forgive. God sees us just the way we are and offers us Jesus to perfect all of our imperfections.

CALL TO ACTION

Do you feel like you are constantly failing in many things? Are you constantly falling into the same sin and temptation? Know that Christ is faithful to forgive you in the midst of your failures. This is the perfect picture of God's incredible grace towards you and me. He gave His Son to meet our needs. He gave His Son to forgive us. God is a God of second chances. Because God is love and His love is given to you in the cross of Jesus Christ. Ponder some of your shortcomings. Write them down and ask God to forgive you. Know that you are forgiven in Christ.

*"God sees us just the way we are and offers us Jesus
to perfect all of our imperfections."*

Absolute Obedience

Jonah obeyed the word of the Lord and went to Nineveh. Now Nineveh was a very large city; it took three days to go through it. Jonah began by going a day's journey into the city, proclaiming, "Forty more days and Nineveh will be overthrown." The Ninevites believed God. A fast was proclaimed, and all of them, from the greatest to the least, put on sackcloth.

JONAH 3:3–5

Every person is created in a unique way—but isn't it interesting that we are uniformly disobedient? What makes our disobedience so evident is that we have a largely uniform understanding what is wrong and what is right, i.e. morals. This disobedience, or moral failure, is often a direct result of our sinful tendencies.

Jonah, a sinful being, disobeyed God in the first chapter of the narrative. But here we find ourselves in chapter three and Jonah's response was a little different this time. Verse three states, "Jonah obeyed the word of the Lord and went to Nineveh" (Jonah 3:3). His obedience was a result of encountering God in a personal way. He knew the great God that he was serving. Jonah went to Nineveh, proclaiming God's message to the people. And because of Jonah's obedience in sharing God's message, many Ninevites believed in God (Jonah 3:5).

God created mankind in His very image (Genesis 1:27), but we decided to disobey Him from the beginning because we wanted to outsmart God, which resulted in our selfish pursuit of self-gratification. We see in the Genesis account, how man and woman disobeyed God's command to not eat of the tree of the knowledge of good and evil (Genesis 2:17; 3:6–7). Disobedience is now at the core of our human nature—especially our disobedience towards God. Jonah, a disobedient prophet, could encounter God in a profound way. This encounter allowed him to see that God is bigger than his disobedience, and that God will use him regardless of his disobeying ways. This same God is yearning to encounter us in a profound way. Even in our disobedience towards Him, God is longing to forgive us, just as he forgave Jonah. This forgiveness ultimately comes through God's very own Son, Jesus Christ.

CALL TO ACTION

Have you ever wondered where God is calling you? While we often feel certain that He is calling us to a vocation, life decision, or location, God is ultimately calling us to Himself. Christian, find your refuge and strength in Christ alone. In your uncertainties and doubts, God is calling you to cling to Him. This is absolute obedience: Christ paid the price for your sin, died, resurrected, and ascended to God's right hand. And in Christ, your disobedience is redeemed and perfected before God. Seek first the kingdom of God (Matthew 6:33), then incline your ear and listen, as God leads you where He wants to take you.

REFLECTIONS ON JONAH 3:3-5

"Even in our disobedience towards Him,
God is longing to forgive us."

Responding to God

When Jonah's warning reached the king of Nineveh, he rose from his throne, took off his royal robes, covered himself with sackcloth and sat down in the dust. This is the proclamation he issued in Nineveh: "By the decree of the king and his nobles: Do not let people or animals, herds or flocks, taste anything; do not let them eat or drink. But let people and animals be covered with sackcloth. Let everyone call urgently on God. Let them give up their evil ways and their violence. Who knows? God may yet relent and with compassion turn from his fierce anger so that we will not perish."

JONAH 3:6–9

Do you ever get important phone calls that need to be answered, yet somehow you happen to miss them? This is true with many of us. It is not always an easy thing to catch every phone call as it comes. But when we do answer the phone, we know exactly how important a certain call may be.

In these next few verses, there are multiple responses to God's command. God asked Jonah to preach against Nineveh due to its wickedness. Jonah's warning reached its way to the king of Nineveh. As the king of Nineveh heard God's warning against him and his people, he removed his royal robes, covered himself with sackcloth—a symbol of repentance and mourning—and sat in the dust. The king issued a decree to the city stating, "*Do not let people or animals, herds or flocks, taste anything; do not let them eat or drink. But let people and animals be covered with sackcloth. Let everyone call urgently on God. Let them give up their evil ways and their violence. Who knows? God may yet relent and with compassion turn from his fierce anger so that we will not perish*" (Jonah 3:7–9). It was clear that God's message was sent to Nineveh through Jonah. This prompted the second response, the response of the king of Nineveh. The king heard God's message being proclaimed through Jonah and responded to it by repenting of his city's wrongdoing.

When God is trying to get our attention, we often look away. As we have seen throughout Jonah's journey, he too, looked away. In our looking away, we put in danger our ability to hear from God. When God speaks, He wants us to respond—just as when we speak to God and want a response from Him. God called Jonah to respond, Jonah disobeyed, and God paved a way for Jonah to think on his actions. Jonah realized what he had done and repented of his sinful actions. In a similar fashion, the city of Nineveh was living in wickedness. God's message was sent to the king through Jonah, and the king repented of the disobedience that permeated the city. God heard the king's response, and did not bring the destruction that He had threatened (Jonah 3:10). So how do we respond to God in the times that He is speaking to us? We respond to God in repentance and faith, believing what He is saying is true. We do this not on our own doing, but on what has already been done for us in the gospel. Christ has conquered sin. And because of this, we are able to understand our need to repent in response to God. God will get through to us in our repentant hearts. But if we are living in our unrepentant sin, then it will be difficult to hear God, and even more so, it will be difficult to respond to God.

CALL TO ACTION

Spend some time dwelling on Christ's work for you on the cross. Jesus' body was broken and His blood was shed for you. Reflect on this. Confess any unrepentant sins that you may have. Respond to what God has taught you today.

REFLECTIONS ON JONAH 3:6-9

"Respond to God in repentance and faith,
believing what He is saying is true."

A Faithful God

When God saw what they did and how they turned from
their evil ways, he relented and did not bring on them the
destruction he had threatened.

Jonah 3:10

Faithfulness is not easy. We constantly fall into sin, just as the
people of Nineveh did. We search to fulfill the desires of our
flesh, rather than surrendering to our faithful God. How are you
missing the mark in being faithful to God and His purposes? Are
you like the people of Nineveh prior to hearing Jonah's rebuke?

God honors obedience and faithfulness. Because of the Nin-
evite king's obedience to God's message, God relented and did
not bring destruction upon the people of Nineveh. God's message
commandeered the hearts and minds of the Ninevites, and God
continued to be faithful in providing the needs of His people.

No matter our faithlessness, God will always remain faithful. It is His very character. Throughout the entirety of the Old
Testament, God tested and tried His unfaithful people, Israel. In
their unfaithfulness, God remained faithful to His covenant promises. God has made us, the Church, a faithful covenant promise in

His Son, Jesus Christ. This promise is life everlasting, which can only be found in Christ (John 3:16; John 14:6). As we continue to be God's unfaithful people, He will continue to call us faithful in and through Christ Jesus. This is the power of the gospel. The gospel makes us whole. The gospel encourages us to look to Christ amid our failures and shortcomings. He is faithful to forgive us in Christ. When in doubt, hold on to our firm foundation. Hold on to our cornerstone. Hold on to our all in all, who is Jesus. And when you fail, God will pour out His overwhelming grace, because He is faithful.

CALL TO ACTION

Rejoice. Rejoice in our faithful God. Rejoice in the gospel of Christ. This very gospel is the reason we live and breathe. This very gospel is given freely to you by the same God who spared the destruction of Nineveh. God is faithful. He is just. He is merciful. Do you believe in His faithfulness? Spend some time writing. Thank God for the gospel. Reflect on His faithfulness.

REFLECTIONS ON JONAH 3:10

"He will continue to call us faithful
in and through Christ Jesus."

PART 4

Jonah Chapter Four

Righteous Anger

But to Jonah this seemed very wrong, and he became angry. He prayed to the Lord, "Isn't this what I said, Lord, when I was still at home? That is what I tried to forestall by fleeing to Tarshish. I knew that you are a gracious and compassionate God, slow to anger and abounding in love, a God who relents from sending calamity. Now, Lord, take away my life, for it is better for me to die than to live." But the Lord replied, "Is it right for you to be angry?"

JONAH 4:1–4

We have all been angry. But how often is our anger righteous, i.e. honoring to God? Anger is a gift from God. He created us to have emotions so that we could put them on display. How we put them on display is a matter of righteous emotions or sinful emotions. The reality is that we hardly display genuine righteous anger which results in an anger that is led by sin.

Jonah did not respond well to Nineveh's response to God's message. Jonah was angry because he did not want the Ninevites to repent of their wickedness towards God—because he wanted them to burn for their sins. He was angry and did not want to preach to them because his hatred for them had grown exceedingly. The Ninevites responded in great obedience to God's message and they showed hearts of change and hearts of repentance. Jonah began praying to God, letting his emotions show. He reaffirmed to God that he knew that He was a compassionate God, who is slow to anger and abounding in love, and a God who relents from sending calamity. Jonah was so frustrated at the response of the Ninevites, that he had told God in his prayer that he would rather die than live much longer. He felt that his proclamation of God's truth should have triggered a different response, rather than God's relenting on the Ninevites deserved punishment.

How often do we set expectations before us, God intervenes and redirects us, and we become angry with God? It seems that there may be a little bit of Jonah in all of us. But when we become angry with God, is it a righteous anger? Often times, we do not bring about righteous anger because we are indeed, sinful people. And sinful people do not have the might to produce righteous anger. But how can we acquire a genuine, righteous, God-honoring anger? We must look to the cross. Righteous anger is found at the cross. Christ Himself experienced anger. And when He did, He displayed it without sin. He displayed righteous anger. Christ took our unrighteous anger and put it to death on the cross. He redeemed it. He purified it. When we are angry, let us take our anger to the cross, asking God to purify it in His Son.

CALL TO ACTION

Are you on the verge of unrighteous anger? Are you already there? Take your anger to the feet of Jesus. Rest in Him. Allow Him to sanctify your anger for the glory of God. Spend some time journaling about what is causing you to be. If you are not angry, allow God to prompt you to encourage someone who is.

REFLECTIONS ON JONAH 4:1-4

*"Christ took our unrighteous anger and
put it to death on the cross."*

Loving Father

Jonah had gone out and sat down at a place east of the city.
There he made himself a shelter, sat in its shade and waited
to see what would happen to the city. Then the Lord God
provided a leafy plant and made it grow up over Jonah to
give shade for his head to ease his discomfort, and Jonah
was very happy about the plant.

JONAH 4:5–6

Love is a word that is overused in its improper understanding. Often-times, we think of love as a feeling that we get for
someone, and this feeling cannot be explained or understood. We
then chase after this feeling as if the solution to it is simply telling
the person that we love them. In doing so, we eagerly wait to hear
the same response back. Once our love is requited, we believe that
love has been fulfilled. But is love just a feeling that we take at face
value, or is love more of a gift that we receive?

After Jonah made his anger known to God, he went east
of Nineveh. He made a shelter and sat down in the shade as he
observed the city, waiting to see if something would happen. As

Jonah waited, God provided him with a leafy plant which shaded Jonah's head from the blazing sun.

What compelled God to provide this plant for Jonah? Why would God give something so pleasant for Jonah, after Jonah just spewed words of anger towards God? The answer is love. Love is the reason that God comforted Jonah. Love is God's very nature. Jonah did nothing to deserve the shade, but in His grace, God took care of Jonah because He is a loving Father. Fortunately for us we don't just encounter God's feelings towards us, although these are vital, but we experience His love through action. And this gift is absolutely free. God, in His love, has given us His Son, Jesus Christ, as Salvation, paying the penalty of our sins by dying on the cross, so that we may live forever (John 3:16). We do nothing to deserve the wondrous gift of the gospel. The gift of perfect love can only be given by a perfect and holy God. God's love wasn't only spoken about, but it was acted upon. And God offers it to us so that we may receive the gift of true love. This is a love that can never be taken away, because Jesus has already paid the penalty for sin on our behalf. God is not here to judge you, but to save you. So how do we receive this gift from our loving Father in heaven? We simply believe that God loved us so much that He gave His one and only Son, who gives us life everlasting.

CALL TO ACTION

Brothers and sisters, know this: your heavenly Father cares for you. He cares for you to the point of death. He sacrificed His One and Only Son, Jesus Christ, in order to pay for the penalty of sin. In Christ, your sin is wiped clean. When God looks at you, He sees Jesus. This is because our God is a loving Father. He cares about you. He cares about what you're going through. He wants you to come to Him and receive. Receive the gift of love offered to you in Christ Jesus.

"The gift of perfect love can only be given by a perfect and holy God."

Desire to Give Up

But at dawn the next day God provided a worm, which chewed the plant so that it withered. When the sun rose, God provided a scorching east wind, and the sun blazed on Jonah's head so that he grew faint. He wanted to die, and said, "*It would be better for me to die than to live.*" But God said to Jonah, "Is it right for you to be angry about the plant?" "It is," he said. "And I'm so angry I wish I were dead."

JONAH 4:7–9

Are you in a place where you want to give up? Giving up may be the easiest thing that you can do. You simply stop doing something and quit. We can give up on many things in life. We can give up on our careers, on playing sports, on exercising, eating healthy, and dieting. Or one can simply give up on life—decide to sit at home and do absolutely nothing. What could be the most dangerous though, is the possibility of giving up on God.

Jonah experienced firsthand the desire to give up. Even in the midst of God's provision for Jonah, Jonah did not see the love that God had for him. To Jonah, it was better to be angry than to receive God's love. Here, God decides to test Jonah by sending a worm to eat up the plant so that it may wither. Not only that, but God provided a scorching east wind, and caused the sun to blaze on Jonah's head. As this occurred, Jonah's response was striking. Jonah said, "It would be better for me to die than to live" (Jonah 4:8). Jonah had enough. He just wanted to give up and die. Jonah also believed that it was right to be angry about the plant, even though the plant was a gift from God in the first place—angry enough to want to die.

How many of us have been in Jonah's shoes? When we are overwhelmed, stressed out, or frustrated, we lean towards a tendency to just give up. But when we look at the incarnate Christ, He too, dealt with some of the most excruciating pain and devastating frustration. He prayed to His Father in heaven many times, asking Him to rid Him of certain sufferings. Yet Christ would always follow those prayers with, "Not My will but Yours be done" (Luke 22:42). Despite the difficulty of His life, Jesus rested in the arms of God the Father Almighty. Christian, are you weary and heavy laden? If so, rest in the gospel of Jesus Christ. For He promises to give you rest (Matthew 11:28). When you desire to give up, just as Jonah did, Christ will give you all that you need to conquer your desire. Trust in Him. Believe that He will grant you the peace that will encourage you to keep going. In Christ alone, our hope is found. Rest in your precious Savior, who longs to give you rest when you desire to give up.

CALL TO ACTION

Take a moment to write down some things that are leading you to give up. No matter what it may be, know that Christ gives you peace. Christ will give you the strength to get through. Rest in His unchanging grace and trust in the merciful gospel that meets you no matter your circumstances. And trust in Christ to get you through, even when you desire to give up.

REFLECTIONS ON JONAH 4:7–9

*"When you desire to give up, Christ will give you
all that you need to conquer your desire."*

God's Care for His People

But the Lord said, "You have been concerned about this plant, though you did not tend it or make it grow. It sprang up overnight and died overnight. And should I not have concern for the great city of Nineveh, in which there are more than a hundred and twenty thousand people who cannot tell their right hand from their left—and also many animals?"

JONAH 4:10-11

We care about many things in this world. We care about our statuses, the trajectory of our careers, who our friends are, our families. We care about our income. We care about our favorite sports teams. All this to say: we were made to be caring people. But is our care focused in the wrong places? Do we spend our time caring for things that we could do without? What do you care about? What about being cared for? We delight in being taken care of by others. When someone expresses their care for us, we are humbled by the fact that someone else might choose to go out of their way on our behalf.

Jonah was concerned about the plant and was frustrated when it withered. This is because Jonah was self-absorbed, thinking only about his needs. But care is not about the self. It is about the needs of others. Throughout the narrative, Jonah seems to always focus on himself. God, on the other hand, has no equal when it comes to caring for others. When Jonah is busy focusing on his (perceived) needs and desires, God offers His gracious care for Jonah and the people of Nineveh. As Jonah sits and observes the people of Nineveh out of curiosity of what was going to transpire, God provides the Ninevites with the freedom that is offered in Himself. As Jonah pouts to God, God tells Jonah that He cares for the city of Nineveh and its people.

Our care is not righteous. It is selfish. Most of the time when we care for others we are thinking of ourselves. And in moments when we need to be cared for, it seems like no one is available to meet our needs. God, however, cares for His people. God's most powerful and incredible care is displayed in the gospel. He cares to the point of dying on the cross for you and me. God saw brokenness which causes sin—our separation from God—and He cared for us by sending His Son, to redeem us of our sin. Christ paid the price that we ought to pay. This price was paid because God wanted to restore His relationship with humanity, because He is a caring God. Though the Ninevites were living in a way that was contrary to God and His standards, God, in His care, spared their lives so that they may know Him. He does the same for us. He does this in the gospel of Christ Jesus.

CALL TO ACTION

Spend some time reflecting on the care that is freely given to you from God in Christ. Every burden, pain, and sorrow is swallowed into the grace and mercy of our Lord Jesus Christ. He cares for you; He longs to be in relational union with you, so that He may offer you the care that your spirit truly longs for. Jesus cared for all that He encountered throughout His earthly ministry and asks you to cast all of your anxieties on Him, because He cares for you (1

Peter 5:7). Do you trust Him to comfort you? Will you surrender your burdens upon Him? Spend time casting your cares upon the Lord for He is faithful to forgive and purify.

"He cares to the point of dying on the cross for you and me."

Conclusion

If there is anything that we can learn from the story of Jonah it's that God is a God of unending grace. His grace is both deep and profound. Right from the get go, God expresses His loving grace to the sailors on the ship with Jonah. He reveals Himself to them through Jonah's disobedience. Then God shows His grace to Jonah by providing a large fish that swallows him, which spares his life from being in deep water. God forgives Jonah for his disobedience and He pours out His grace on Jonah yet again when the large fish vomits Jonah out onto dry land. This time, Jonah proclaims God's message to a wicked people, the Ninevites. In this proclamation, we see the grace of God extended towards the people of Nineveh. They were living in wickedness, yet God, in His grace, offered them a way out of their sin. God is love, and God is a God of second chances. The narrative of Jonah shows God's grace towards us. We fail him time and time again, just as Jonah did. Just as the sailors did. Just like the Ninevites did prior to hearing his word. But even in the midst of all this failure to measure up to God's standards, God cared for the sailors, the Ninevites, and Jonah. His grace is sufficient, even when His people fall short.

This is the gospel narrative; We as Christians fail God time and time again, yet God in Christ, gives us hope. The gospel of Christ Jesus sets us free and this freedom allows us to experience the depths of God's love for us. My hope is that you have experienced the riches of God's restoring grace throughout the Jonah narrative, and in your own personal life. May you be blessed in Him who is able to conquer all things through the power of the gospel, which is freely given to you by faith.

Small Group Study Questions

JONAH CHAPTER ONE

Stop Running, Listen (Jonah 1:1–3)

1. What do you think is at the core of our tendency to run away from God?

2. Jonah ran away from God because he was in fear of what God was asking Him to do. Do you ever fear what God may be asking you to do for Him? What is your fear rooted in?

3. How can you resolve the tension of choosing to run towards God, even when you're not experiencing that desire?

4. How can understanding God's restoring grace change the way you listen to Him?

5. How can understanding God's restoring grace change your habit of running from Him?

In the Midst of Storms (1:4–6)

1. Share about the storms that you have gone through in your life.

2. When storms arrive, how do you handle them?

3. Can you possibly handle the storms in your life in a better way? If so, how?

4. How does your view of God change the way you approach the storms in your life?

5. How can drawing near to God change your attitude in the midst of storms?

Identity (1:7–9)

1. What defines your identity?

2. Describe how your view of identity changes the way you live?

3. Do you find your identity in your job description? How so?

4. How can you allow God to reshape the way that you think about your identity?

5. How can you change the way you think about your identity in Christ?

Our Need for God (1:10–12)

1. How are you able to make time for God in your busyness?

2. What is the biggest challenge about spending alone time with God?

3. What area of your life do you need God most?

4. Does your need for God change the way you live each day? How?

5. How can you fully embrace your need for God?

A Life without Godliness Is a Life of Tragedy (1:13–16)

1. Do you ever live as if God is abstract? Explain.

2. How does a perception of an abstract God change the way you live?

3. What are some aspects in your life that consist of godlessness?

4. What are some things that you can do to pursue godliness?

God's Sovereign Provision (1:17)

1. What are some things that you attempt to control in your life?

2. What steps do you need to take in order to release control of these things?

3. Does it bring you comfort knowing that God cares about your needs? If yes, how so?

4. What is the cause of neglecting God's sovereign provision for your life?

5. What step(s) can you take in order to trust God with the provision that He has for you?

JONAH CHAPTER TWO

In My Distress (2:1–2)

1. What are some things that bring you distress?

2. How do you handle distress?

3. What are some ways that you could remove the distresses of your life?

4. In what ways would your life be different if you gave your distresses unto the Lord?

The Power of Lament (2:3–5)

1. How do you perceive lament?

2. Why do you think many Christians shy away from lament?

3. How do you think lament is glorifying to God?

4. When was the last time you spent time lamenting?

5. How can lamenting nourish your faith in God?

Worship (2:6–9)

1. What does worship mean to you?

2. What are some idols in your life that you worship which push you away from God?

3. How do different styles of worship impact your relationship with God?

4. What are some changes in your habits that you need to make in order to worship God more?

5. How can the way you worship grow your relationship with Christ?

JONAH CHAPTER THREE

Second Chances (2:10—3:2)

1. When have you experienced a second chance in life?

2. How did that second chance change you?

3. How have you seen God give you a second chance?

4. What emotions have you encountered, knowing that God offers an unlimited supply of second chances?

5. How can you live knowing that God has healed you and has given you a second chance?

Absolute Obedience (3:3–5)

1. What does obedience mean to you?

2. Have you struggled with obeying God? How so?

3. What are the implications of disobeying God?

4. How can you change your posture and pursue absolute obedience?

5. How can absolute obedience transform the way you think about God?

Responding to God (3:6–9)

1. When was a time that God was asking you of something, yet you did not respond?

2. What is the biggest challenge in responding to what God is asking of you?

3. Share a time when you called out to God and He responded to you?

4. How can that experience change the way you respond to God?

5. What can you do differently in order to respond to God when He is asking something of you?

A Faithful God (3:10)

1. Share a time when you experienced the faithfulness of God.

2. What allowed you to see His faithfulness?

3. How does God's faithfulness change the way you live?

4. What are some ways that you can resemble God's faithfulness to others?

5. When you are not aware of God's faithfulness, how can you still know that He is faithful?

JONAH CHAPTER FOUR

Righteous Anger (4:1–4)

1. How do you handle anger?
2. How often is your anger righteous?
3. How can you transform your sinful anger into righteous anger?
4. What are some ways that you could encourage others dealing with anger issues?
5. How can anger be righteous?

Loving Father (4:5–6)

1. How have you encountered the love of God?
2. What are the implications of God's love for us in Christ?
3. How does God's love for you shape the way you live?
4. What are some ways that you can share the love of God with others?
5. How can you display God's love in your daily environment?

Desire to Give Up (4:7–9)

1. When was a time that you felt like giving up?
2. How did you get through that time?
3. Do you still struggle with giving up sometimes? How so?
4. What is the cause of your desire to give up?
5. How can your relationship with God impact your desire to give up?

God's Care for His People (4:10–11)

1. What does care mean to you?

2. How do you display care in your daily life?

3. How does God's care for you change the way that you live?

4. How can you care for others in light of God's care for you?

5. What can you do this week to show God's care for others?